John W. Walton,

D0629260

WITHDRAWN

Alfred J LaBelle
BOOKS
STATIONERY
GIFTS
IRMINGHAM – MICHIGAN

OPUS 7

821
W247o

SYLVIA TOWNSEND WARNER

OPUS 7

NEW YORK

THE VIKING PRESS

1931

COPYRIGHT, 1931, BY THE VIKING PRESS, INC.

PRINTED IN THE UNITED STATES OF AMERICA
BY QUINN & BODEN

To

ARTHUR MACHEN

132047

OPUS 7

OPUS 7

"ERE I descend into the grave,
let me a small house and large garden have."
So Cowley wished; and if he could have seen
Rebecca Random's cottage at Love Green
he would have cried: " 'Tis here!" Deep thatch it had,
large beams, small windows, all things such as glad
the hearts of those who dwell in town but would
spend weekends in the country; strangers stood
admiring it, cars stopped, Americans
levelled their cameras, and a painter once
sat for two days beside a pigsty wall
to take a picture of it, though as all
agreed who took a passing squint, his view
was Bedlam-work, all daubs, red spots and blue,
mingling with white unearthly atomies
where drawers and nightgowns hung to better eyes.

3

Nor did folk only gaze. Many enquired
how old Rebecca was, or if she hired
out furnished rooms in summer. Sure, they said,
so aged a woman only needs a bed
and a back-kitchen. She can cook, maybe;
our wants are few: breakfast, lunch, dinner, tea,
beds made, rooms cleaned, our laundry now and again
(we see she launders). . . . They enquired in vain;
Rebecca lodged nor let, nor would she hear
of sale—'twas freehold—though an auctioneer
came in his Austin Seven from the town
proffering fifty guineas, money down.
Neighbours discussing this across the fence
declared her foolish, but approved her sense;
for fifty guineas, though a weighty sum,
so headlong gained is bound to be *Light come,
Light go*, while fifty guineas safe refused
is yours for ever, virgin and unused,
a fortune none can filch, deny, or spend,
undimmable boast, and credit without end.

Leave we the house and walk the garden round:
a good half-acre, and old orchard ground;

4

in all Love Green the easiest soil—a mould
sweetened with ending of sweet lives untold.
Blossom and leaf and twig and windfall were
mixed in that gentle lap; time did inter
his summers there, and bade them rot in peace,
natural resurrection, due increase
promising, and continuance of green
out of their sere. But now few trees were seen,
and they, lopped back; as rare and circumscribed
as kings in Europe now those trees survived,
and to the spring a shrunken blooth put out,
by few bees visited, for all about
Their feet a new democracy displayed
livelier assurances of richer trade.

Here at Old Christmas bloomed the Christmas rose,
true to her date however man dispose
the calendar, here velvet wallflowers bloomed,
and with attempting breath March gales perfumed
from their male chastity almost; snowdrops and squills
limned April skies below while yet the hills
rose into mist, while yet the shepherd blew
warm on the lamb beside the quaking ewe.

5

Here, when the lamb leaped gleaming in the sun,
was mustered such a garden garrison
as tale outnumbered, penny packet's show
outshone; but not, like Marvell's, ranked in row,
drilled under colours, marshalled for parade—
these a more unsophisticated fusillade
loosed off, hubbub of shape and hue and scent,
a countrified militia, where intent
is to be foremost all, most willing each.
Rebecca was no Frederick, to teach
austerer discipline; they throve, said she,
as children do, by mixing company;
one countenanced another, and the soil
was plenty good enough for none to moil.
And should some wilding outlaw, long decreed
by due botanical consent a weed,
to her tilled ground come interloping back,
let it but bloom, she would not bid it pack.
Bloom did they all, the bond beside the free,
true clove carnation neighbouring succory,
Ishmaelite poppy with delphinium;
it seemed the Eden or Millennium

6

of flowers, how all at peace together grew:
the feckless, well-apparelled lily-crew,
yet gay in gospel since they chanced to please
Christ on his rambles, lived not more at ease.
Nor did their mistress labour overmuch.
Some skill she had, and, more than skill, a touch
that prospered all she set, as though there were
a chemical affinity 'twixt her
stuff and the stuff of plants—a pulse, a stroke,
implicit in her grubbing paws, that woke
the dreaming seed, and bade the root take hold;
an Open Sesame of the hand, that old
west-country parlance knows as "a green thumb."
  "Rebecca do have luck with flowers," quoth some,
glancing across the hedge, while others mocked
to see so rich a ground so idly stocked.
But praise and blame had other fish to fry,
and aimed on their own cares went careless by.
It was the children who delayed. To them
Rebecca's garden was the diadem
of all Love Green; not even the churchyard,
with rivalry of elegiac jam-pots, hard-

frozen lilies and roses under glass,
and the new war memorial could surpass
it as a gazing-stock and raree-show.
More it was not—how much more, being so!—
A prohibition in the first-devised
garden that paradise emparadised,
which slighted, all was common as elsewhere:
so here, to those unfallen without, there were
no weeds, no toil, no curse, save the well-known
shrill threat of "Drat you, leave my gate alone!"
Over that gate they leaned in long survey,
and stared as though at India or Cathay.
There were the flowers; pampered, secure, and calm
as turbanned sultans underneath a palm,
they in their usurped territory reigned,
and with renewing pomps their pomp sustained,
flaunting their privacy, confederate
but with themselves; and there, with lumbering gait,
Rebecca, stooped and stout and red of face,
moved like the guardian goblin of their race—
herself no flower. Yet this disparity
seemed more contrivance than fortuity,

a stroke of art, a discord shrewdly set;
her foulness to their favour matched well-met,
as ogres elves corroborate in fables.

But where, you ask, where were the vegetables?—
the dues each rustic from however clenched
soil should extort—potatoes duly trenched,
the buxom cabbage, onions well-trod,
and marrows rounding to the glory of God
at harvest festival—you name not these.
They were not. Save those wizened apple trees,
whose windfalls only wasp and ant found sweet,
this garden offered nothing one could eat.
Fie, fie, indeed! How wanton and perverse!
Grow only flowers?—as well write only verse!
And in so good a soil? Were but this realm
an honest Soviet, judgment would o'erwhelm
her and her trumpery, and the freehold give
to brisker hands. How did the woman live?
You called her stout. I'd like to see her thin,
then she'd find out if flowers pad bones from skin.
Rebecca lived on bread, and lived for gin.

WHEN grandees feasted have, to see the abhorred
heeltaps and damaged dainties to the board
come cringing back agrees not with their taste—
eat they will not, and yet they would not waste.
Then to the butler's or the cook's discreet
beck comes the charwoman on stealthy feet,
and in a bag receives, and bears away,
the spoiling relics of a splendid day.
Time bears (my Lord) just such a bag, and deft-
handed is he to pouch whatever's left
from bygone exploits when their glories fail.
I knew a time when Europe feasted well:
bodies were munched in thousands, vintage blood
so blithely flowed that even the dull mud
grew greedy, and ate men; and lest the gust
should flag, quick flesh no daintier taste than dust,
spirit was ransacked for whatever might
sharpen a sauce to drive on appetite.
From the mind's orient fetched all spices were—
honour, romance, magnanimous despair,
savagery, expiation, lechery,
skill, humour, spleen, fear, madness, pride, ennui....

Long revel, but at last to loathing turned,
and through the after-dinner speeches yawned
those who still waked to hear them. No one claps.
Come, Time, 'tis time to bear away the scraps!
    Time came, and bent him to the priestlike task.
Once more Love Green beheld its farmers bask
in former ruin; homecome heroes, badged
with native mud, to native soil repledged
limbs that would lose their record, ten years hence,
whether they twinged for tillage or defence.
No longer was the church on weekdays warmed
that special liturgies might be performed;
war-babies, too, now lost their pristine glamour,
and were as bastards bid to hold their clamour.
So Time dispatched the feast; some items still
surpassed his pouch, though; one of these, the bill.
Many, for this, the hind who pinched and numb
faced the wet dawn, and thought of army rum;
many the mother, draggled from childbed,
who wept for grocer's port and prices fled;
and village Hampdens, gathered in the tap,
forsook their themes of bawdry and mishap

to curse a government which could so fleece
on spirits under proof, and call it Peace.
    And thus it was Rebecca came to grow
sweet flowers, and only flowers. War trod her low.
Her kin all dead, alas! too soon had died;
unpensioned, unallowanced, unsupplied
with pasteboard window-boast betokening
bloody-money sent from a respectful king,
she on her freehold starved, the sullen bait
of every blithe philosopher on fate.
Dig she could not. Where was the farmer who
would hire her sodden limbs when well he knew
how shapely landgirls, highbred wenches all,
would run in breeches at his beck and call?
To beg would be in vain. What patriot purse
would to a tippler open, when its terse
clarion call the *Daily Mail* displayed:
Buckingham Palace Drinking Lemonade?
So fared she worsening on, until the chimes
clashing out peace, renewal of old times—
but bettered—sent her stumbling to the inn.
No! No reduction in the price of gin.

A crippled Anzac saw her. "Here, I'll treat
the lady. What's your fancy? Take it neat?
Say, here's the lousy peace they talk about!"
The fire so long unfelt ran like a shout
of Alleluias all along her blood.
Reared out of her indignities she stood
weeping·for joy. The soldier looked, and laughed,
and poured another, and again she quaffed,
and a third time. It was a rousing drink;
through weeks to come it did her good to think
it had been hers—long weeks of misery,
cold, influenza, charitable tea.
And in the spring he came once more; still lame,
not brown now, emptied of his mirth, he came,
and leaned across her gate. "Those flowers you call
wallflowers . . . I'd like a few." She gave him all.

Mute and intent he turned them in his hand.
She watched them, too, and could not understand
what charm held him thus steadfast to a thing
that just bloomed out by nature every spring.
At last he spoke, though not so much to her
as to all things around. "My great-grandfer

13

was bred up hereabouts; and here he courted
his girl, and married her, and was transported
for firing ricks, and left the girl behind.
He picked a young she-convict to his mind,
and settled down, and got a family.
He told my grand-dad, he my dad, him, me,
all about England. When I was a pup
I felt to come to England I'd give up
all I could ever have—and here I am,
her soldier. Now, I wouldn't give a damn
for England. She's as rotten as a cheese,
her women bitches, and her men C 3's.
This silly soppy landscape—what's the use
of all this beauty and no bloody juice?
Who'd fire a rick in these days?" "Farmer Lee
fired his for the insurance once," said she.
He heard not, and spoke on. "I've come too late,
and stay too long. Ruin can fascinate
a man like staring in a cattle-hole;
that still, black water-look pulls down his soul.
England is getting hold of me. That's why
I asked you for those flowers. Good luck! Good-bye."

He turned away, and turned again, and slid
a paper in her hand. When she undid
its crumples she was clutching a pound note.
The liquor seemed already in her throat.
Quick! To the inn! And yet she still delayed.
Strange thoughts worked in her mind. She watched
        them braid
themselves into an order, vivify
into a scheme, blossom, a policy.
As some on liquor, some on flowers were set;
would pay, too, witness this; each violet
crushed drop by drop into a glass would spill
its farthing, ha'penny, pennyworth, until
the glass brimmed to her stooping lips. Why then,
grow flowers, sell flowers, buy liquor—so, Amen!

Dull is despair. As well sharpen a knife
on lead, as wits on wanhope; the sole life-
blood of all cunning, spur of every plan,
is hope; hope makes the Machiavellian.
Up at the inn Rebecca half displayed,
half hid, the miracle. "Oh, yes, I paid
twelve-and-six for the bottle, money down . . .

a wicked price!" She toyed with half-a-crown.
"This here king's head be pretty, don't you think?"
Nearer they drew, and hoped she'd stand a drink
(she did not), and, a thirstier hope than this,
hoped she'd tell more. "They have not come amiss,
these warm spring days. My wallflowers are a show.
Were, I should say, for but an hour ago
I sold them to a foreign gentleman.
Soon the co-operative will send their van
Tuesdays as well as Fridays, so I hear,
and Mrs. Bulley's other leg is queer."
She rose, and left them gazing in their beer.

ENOUGH was said. Before the celandine
opened to the next sunrise, all Love Green
welcomed this wonder risen in their east,
and to amazement sat, as to a feast.
Two-headed monsters are the natural diet
of those pure minds which dwell in country quiet—
sustenance never lacked, where dullness sways
with earthy sceptre the farm labourer's days.

16

Blest fertile Dullness! mothering surmise,
rumour, report, as stagnant water, flies,
whose happy votaries, stung by every hatch,
divinely itch, and more divinely scratch!
Nothing's too wild for credence, or too slight
for fancy to apparel it in light
fetched from the half-wit moon: a gatepost can,
if rightly studied, feed the mind of man
with a rich entertainment; an old goat
more plenteous bawdry than the French priest wrote
bequeath, sprat wag more waves than any whale;
but, best of all, strangers deck out a tale.
    Trade on that morrow throve uncommonly.
Each housewife viewed her stores, and found that she
were instantly undone, did she not haste
for Empress washing blue, or salmon paste,
or postal orders, or canary seed.
They stayed at leisure who had come with speed.
The shop was thronged; unheard above the din
the doorbell rang as more came pushing in;
unmarked the painted ship rocked on the tide
of time still ebbing from the morning's pride,

while wet umbrellas, ranged in patience glum,
mixed sullen swamps on the linoleum.
Joy was it in that dawn to be alive;
like a queen bee escaping from the hive
a wonder was abroad. What though Miss Gale,
the sibyl priestess of the royal mail,
for all their offerings, knew no more than they,
or knew, but did not feel inclined to say?—
as devout scientists can from a tooth
enjoy a dinosaur, the quest for truth
scarce checked at this; since fate would not reveal
the stranger whole, they'd run him down piecemeal.
   One, it appeared, had seen him; another, heard
the thunder of his chariot wheels; a third,
scorning this mortal for more inward light,
had dreamed the whole affair last Tuesday night.
A handsome youth. He had a dog with him.
Two dogs. Three dogs. Gentry must have their whim.
Four dogs. His car stood by the vicarage.
No, no, he walked, poor soul, bowed down with age.
A bag he bore. Two bags. Three bags. No doubt
these white slave traffickers do go about;

wenches he sought, no wallflowers. Not at all,
he bought the flowers for his wife's funeral,
and looked near death himself, so pale and wan.
A red-faced man. 'Twas pity he was gone.
    So spoke each one her mind. More sparingly
they of Rebecca spoke, a topic she
past mark of mouth, a hackney whom for pride
no conversationalist would deign bestride,
not worth a word, and barely worth a sneer.
Was this the clod which fate chose out to rear
a headstone in the corner?—was her patch,
with its half dozen listless hens a-scratch,
and rabble of weeds, fit place for chance to sow
and nurse a wonder up incognito?
Beneath few words they hid their discontent,
and a *nil admirari* sanction lent
to this wild thought of flowers exchanged for gold;
resolving inwardly that as they strolled
homeward, they'd pause with stealth and view the scene
where these same well-paid gilliflowers had been.
    View it they did. There was not much to view—
a score of double daffodils, a few

small, chilblain-coloured primroses, the dears
of some flower-fancying matron of past years,
and near them, drooping as abashed, their bright-
starred woodland kin, transplanted overnight.
No matter: it was none of these they eyed,
but the robbed wallflower stock, which testified
the wonder true. What next? The common itch
for relics, palpable tokens that enrich
hearsay to history, and Jack's master drape
in reassuring likeness to Jack's shape
—Shelley, rare soul!—I have his trousers here.
So every dame must have her souvenir;
beg it for choice, but if unbeggable, buy,
steal, have somehow, before the virtue fly
which contact had bestowed, or rival feel
like lust. They were not called upon to steal.
Rebecca, with an air of every day,
was well prepared to tell them what to pay,
mention, advisedly, another's bid,
and vow in the same breath to keep hers hid
who topped it, lest a spouse should grieve to hear
where money went that might have gone on beer;

thus, dealing with them subtly one by one,
made thirty pence. Her commerce was begun.
  Waving the last farewell with silver-crossed
blest hand, she stood in contemplation lost,
with pursed-up lip, and slow exacting gaze
eyeing her ground, as strategist surveys
the dedicated field of victory;
then searched, as for an omen, in the sky.
The day's long rain was past. Vanquished and cowed,
across the west staggered the rearguard cloud,
and paused awhile, and showed its bloodied flank;
then on to the death-looking north, and sank.
Twig, leaf, and blade in the light's evening
dandled a diamond, faintly glittering,
while overhead some stars, distinct and small,
glittered like waterdrops and did not fall.
  O Spring, O virgin of all virgins, how
silent thou art! I have pursued thee now
along so many winters, sought and snuffed
through last year's grass for thee, combing each tuft
to find thy tiny spears that I might prick
my heart on them; ice has not weighed so thick

but I have seen thy blue within its breast:
I have been sure of thee ere others guessed.
In the lean wood, watching, knee-deep in snow,
myself watching a redskin river flow
eastward to the Atlantic, I had yet
eyes to discover thy first ensign set
flickering on a hazel-bush. Gone then
redskin and river; I was home again
in thee, in thee! But when the long pursuit
expires in the achievement, thou art mute.
Each year I find thee as last year thou wert;
hushed, rapt, annunciate—a speechless hurt
trembling on the green sky and from the branch
that thou must bring to green. Oh, how to stanch
the sorrow welling from an April dusk,
that lifts the moon and buoys it like a husk
up the long dark—how treat with this most dear,
most dolorous virgin-mother of the year?
Frustrate I stand before thee, dispossessed,
unaimed, and feel the quickening in my breast
fail, and sigh back again to clod. O Spring,
how silent thou art! I hear the water ring

shallow along the ford, I hear the birds
lancing the air with joy; thou hast no words
for me, and on my lips the question dies.
I know not why I sought thee, nor surmise
what was the ecstasy I could not snatch,
nor ever shall, though at the last I match
my silence against thine, and scatter down
the staff, the cockle shell, the pilgrim gown,
on my last wayfaring to thee waylaid.

    How long this winter night! How far I've strayed
out of its compass, and return how slow
to the sad self I left five hours ago!—
back from spoiled Saugatuck, back from my death.
The ashes on the hearth lift at my breath
but no spark follows them, my movements smite
the sleeping house. How long this winter night!
And down what leagues of darkness must I yet
trudge, stumble, reel, in the wrought mind's retreat;
then wake, remember, doubt, and with the day
that work which in the darkness shone survey,
and find it neither better nor much worse
than any other twentieth-century verse.

Oh, must I needs be disillusioned, there's
no need to wait for spring! Each day declares
yesterday's currency a few dead leaves;
and through all the sly nets poor technique weaves
the wind blows on, whilst I—new nets design,
a sister-soul to my slut heroine,
she to her dram enslaved, and I to mine.

NATURE in town a captive goddess dwells;
man guards, and grilles enclose, her miracles;
the devotees who through her temples pass
with reverence keep off the new-sown grass;
and not a waft of her green kerchief, spring
down sky-forgetting bus routes signalling,
but some heart greets it, some fidelity
awaited, and with love looks back reply.
This is her civic state. On countryside,
goddess too truly to be deified,
she a more real tribute entertains
of endless strategy, mistrust, and pains.
The farmer, slouching by his sodden shocks,
groans her a hymn; the vigilling shepherd knocks

his breast for cold, telling through every joint
a rosary of aches; hoers anoint
her floor with sweat, and the small-holder, sworn
lifelong the same sour clods to grub forlorn,
weighed with reiterated genuflexions, bows,
stiffens, warps earthward, effigy of his vows.
Them, unappeased, the immortal doxy flouts,
with floods in harvest capping seedtime droughts,
paying their toil with the derisive gold
of ragwort, tansy, and corn-marigold,
or, while their ewes breed not and their pigs die,
bidding the mole increase and multiply.
These are her common flouts; these she confers
impartially among her worshippers,
and can be borne; but hardly, when she wills
her absolute whim to manifest, and spills
foison on unlimed acres, comes a guest,
blowsily plenteous, to the harvest feast
of him whom every diligent neighbour mocks,
whose sheep stray with their scab to wholesome flocks,
whose dodders creep, whose seeding thistles are flown
to tended fields, and leers on him alone.

25

Vainly they rail, the righteous Esau tribe—
too wise, too witless to hold out the bribe
no woman can resist: incompetence.
Well for their peace of mind Rebecca's fence
warded sweet flowers, and only flowers, a gear
beneath their envy. With the growing year
a tide of green swept the brown earth and broke
in such a foam of colour as awoke
new being, new ambition, new delight
from the quotidian faculty of sight.
Not hers, but Nature's, was the artifice.
Do as she would, she could not do amiss.
Uprooted in full bloom (and as some said
out of the churchyard furtively conveyed,
for none knew certainly whence came the trove)
pansy and gold-laced polyanthus throve.
A dead geranium from the vicarage
rubbish-heap scavenged had but to engage
root in her mould to start again to life,
and a pot lily, from the farrier's wife
cajoled, speared up though planted upside down.
There was a Woolworth's in the market town—

the Araby Spice Island, Walsinghame
miraculous, of every village dame,
who from its many-breasted mercies drew
the joys of spending and of saving too.
Thither Rebecca went and like a child
hung o'er the tray, believing and beguiled.
Each pictured packet held a sensible hope,
lisping and sliding in its envelope—
such colours, printed bright and sleek as flames,
such flouncing shapes, and starry, and such names!—
Sweet Sultan, Arabis, Virginia Stock,
Godetia, Clarkia, Alyssum, Hollyhock,
Nasturtium, Mignonette, Canary Vine,
and Everlasting Peas, and those, more fine,
which bore such titles as Miss Wilkinson,
Cora, Mnemosyne, and Gonfalon.
      Returning in the carrier's motor van
she sat nid-nod, while conversation ran
blithe as a freshet over ulcered legs,
murders, spring onions, and the price of eggs.
Hesperus, the kind star which bids all home,
lightened that company jolting through the gloam,

loosened each tongue, and mellowed each fatigue;
resolving friend and foe into a league
which in that narrow heaven close-housed should dwell
in idleness like saints to hear and tell,
sitting for ever filled and never tired
in the blest influence of that star attired.
Them, as though God's, the driver's countenance
out of his mirror overlooked with glance
immovable, while they whom he conveyed,
being mortal, but his hinder parts surveyed.
And like a God he, unpetitioned, knew
of each the ending and appointment due,
for each too soon arrived, when she must make
her bustle, and farewelling friends forsake.
But for those yet within, who felt the breath
of evening enter, it was but a death
that the door closed on, and the dusk estranged,
and but one hearer for more heard exchanged;
and loudlier talked the dwindling company,
and life reared up as at a funeral tea.

But now Rebecca, wont to chatter ding-
dong with the merriest, and when drunk to sing,

sat mute and pensive as a maid returned
from meeting love, whose lips have newly learned
silence beneath a kiss. No van saw she,
no burdened neighbours joggling knee to knee,
but a fenced garden where red faces loomed
lusty a pæony bed, or eyeballs bloomed
flax or forget-me-not, or jessamine
muffled a grizzly beard and columbine
dangled its dovecot from a dirty ear.
Then in a flash all these would disappear,
and in a pantry rows of bottles, all
brimful, clinked cheek by jowl, both great and small.
Blest view, whichever way!—blest state to be
thus bearing home her own felicity,
feeling within her lap the future grope
stirring and swelling in its envelope,
foretasting in her soul draughts even now
on their long distillation sped. "I vow
she's drunk as a lord again," neighbours declared,
seeing with what a lost and lofty air
she scrambled out, waving them such adieux
as only emperors or drunks might use.

Quitting the company to become its theme
she reached her gate, still heavy with the dream,
and leaned there, spinning trophies in her mind
of blooms and bottles endlessly entwined.
The dusk had fallen, parenting the dew
under its cloak; uneasy, a wind blew,
bidding mankind go in and lurk at ease. . . .
Hence, ye profane, before Night's mysteries
out of an elder world that must be done
in the consenting absence of the sun.
Now ebbed the tide of waking from its shores:
about her was the sound of closing doors,
and hens shut in, and the last buckets filled,
and homing footsteps on their threshold stilled.
Now waxing on the air invisible
the woodsmoke hovered with a sharper smell
as fires were fed and kettles set to boil.
Unseeingly she watched the darkening soil
suck back the green, the red, the blue, unchild
itself of all the gaudy brood beguiled
out of its bosom by the clasp of day,
save whimpering white from its own being astray;

until at last she stirred, sighed, saw around
but night, and heard her sigh the only sound.
  She lumbered up the path, stooped for the key
under its brick, went in; but presently
came forth again, bearing a lantern lit,
and smiled about to see its presence flit
by bush and tuft and tree with swinging stride,
waking a startled green on every side—
the painted emerald of a theatre bower;
then knelt, and fell to work with all her power.
To sow by lantern light—it was a scene
unpaired in all the annals of Love Green,
flat against nature and good usage, less
act of a wantwit than a sorceress.
Outlandish her vast shadow prowled and stayed—
a rooting bear, a ghoul about her trade—
beheaded, with her rising, into dark.
Birds scolded at her, dogs began to bark,
John Pigeon, reeling home to fight his wife,
checked at the glare, and bellowed out, *The Strife
is o'er, the battle done*, to scare the fiend;
while him forgetting Mrs. Pigeon leaned

out of the bedroom window in her nightgown,
rapt as a saint at gaze, to track the light down.
  As when a single cackle bruits the hawk,
and straightway the whole henrun wakes a-squawk,
word of this wildfire ran the village through.
Casement of casement asked what was ado,
but stayed no answer, since each cared alone
to set on wing some theory of its own.
Those blest with most propinquity declared
Rebecca mad, or held that she prepared
unhallowed grave for an unlicensed birth,
or hoard of buried bottles would unearth.
Those midway souls, who but her shining saw,
propounded fire, or the offended law
arrived with handcuffs on a bicycle;
whilst those who nothing saw, but heard the swell
of hymns devout and holy psalms intoned
in such a voice as but one neighbour owned
were perfectly convinced that Mr. Pigeon
had cut his consort's throat and found religion.
Danger! yelped dog to dog. At Limetree Farm
tin-voiced galeenies furthered the alarm,

and from their windy city roused, out-wheeled
the affronted parliament of rooks, and pealed
their backward-jangled tocsin overhead,
till Parson Drumble in his genial bed
dreamed of church robbers, woke, and slept once
    more.
  Meanwhile Rebecca, placid as the core
of jostling whirlpool, grubbed and grunted on,
bedding Sweet Sultan by Miss Wilkinson,
larkspur by mignonette and arabis.
No ears had she save for the sliding hiss
of seed released into her horny hand—
a drowsing multitudinous murmur, scanned
with tiny lapse and check—nor any care
for other life than that implicit there;
her being so much in future fixed that she
inhabited an anonymity
of time, an ambiguity of day
hollowed from midnight. And as dreams convey
their own penumbra of oblivion, so
she moving with her lantern to and fro
pulled darkness after her, and with such sleight

33

reshaped her wavering world elsewhere, one might
think 'twas her dream, not she, that walked the night.

Odd, that upon the morrow, with no word
blabbed, or hint breathed, all knew what had occurred,
and saw the house unfired, the sinner unwrung,
the martyred wife alive and giving tongue,
with never a backward longing, never a sigh
for nobler prospects with the dark gone by.
Thus banded starlings, in an elder-bush
a-babble, feel a pentecostal push,
rise like a handful of thrown dust, and sweep
mute along air as though they flew in sleep,
and veer as one, by some unbidden bid,
to a new feeding place; but why they did
just so, just then, not even themselves could tell,
nor need they ask, since here, too, they feed well.
Now at this truth intuitively met,
gossip scarce greeted gossip thereon, but set
up a new calf by general consent,
to glister a religious ornament,
a beacon to all minds, a thing to swear by:

Seed sown by night is bound to come up rarely.
Some praised Rebecca's cunning, some her lore;
all recollected well how once before
some other scientist, removed, or dead,
or aunt to a step-brother-in-law, or read
of in the paper, used the midnight hour so,
and gained a golden medal at the flower show.
  In the long dusks, when maidens first delight
to stroll bare-armed, and the first midges bite
and swallows hawk them, it became the mode
to wander musingly along the road
and halt, by chance, beside the garden plot.
Maybe Rebecca with her watering pot
stood there; if so, good manners bade one edge
How-do-you-doing nearer to the hedge,
casting a courteous sheep's-eye undeclared;
if not, one leaned upon the gate and stared.
By the next evening, having grown more bold,
and the latch somehow giving way, behold,
one stood within, admiring as was due
the way these night-sown seedlings always grew.
Then the same delicate combat was rehearsed,

whether fish fly, or angler fish, snap first—
so the wise gudgeon thinks, at any rate;
Rebecca deftly twitching back the bait
with, "Oh, 'tis nothing. And besides, I believe
I promised it to another. I should grieve
to disappoint her, seeing her so set,
and these particular blooms so hard to get."
"There, there," quoth gudgeon, "I won't spoil your
        trade,"
and twiddling in her pocket still delayed,
priced other nosegays, fancied she'd take none—
flowers do but die, when all is said and done,
a foolish ware. "Yet some will pay for them,"
answered Rebecca, stroking down a stem
with a foreclosing gesture that stroked flame
from the poor fish's heart, and left her tame
to the taught melody as a violin.
This was a pleasant way of earning gin:
easy as kiss your hand, and seemly too;
for with her trade Rebecca's credit grew,
and those who lately saw her and disdained
a sot a-thirst, more reverence entertained

for one who paid with such imperial airs
for her own liquor, and might pay for theirs.
    Close to the ground at first her commerce spread:
posies to take on Sunday to the dead,
a sixpenny knot to deck the mantelboard,
or the young breast of Joy, from her abhorred
black dress and apron freed to disembogue
one night a week in a silk blouse from Vogue.
But with the epiphany of her midnight seed
her light was from these grovelling bushels freed,
and waxing with their greenery upthrust
into a higher sphere, a more august
and profitable air. News wrought like barm
when Mrs. Sankey of the Limetree Farm—
she who in winter wrapped herself in furs,
and walked out with two chasing terriers
like any Squire's lady—through the gate
loosing her imps to romp and ruinate,
said with her civillest show of teeth, "I hear
you're selling flowers. I hope they are not dear."
The flowers were hers, and hers extremely cheap.
What simple shepherd would begrudge a sheep

to Pan flockmaster?—and the sacrifice
was eased by knowing she could raise her price
to humbler customers henceforth, and so
recoup the loss from which such gains should flow.

    Drunkards, they say, however they may hap
to fall, earth takes them kindly in her lap;
rock's a down bed to them, and paving stones
receive with deference their unbroken bones;
the sun by noonday, and the winter's night
scathe not, edged tools don't cut them, nor dogs bite,
but wandering unharmed they recreate,
fall as they will, unfallen Adam's state.
A like kind providence now brooded over
Rebecca's steps, even when she was sober.
Her ways were plenteousness, her paths were peace;
all summers, even wet ones, brought increase,
and markets matched themselves to her supply—
as in political economy.
None gave a tea-party or funeral
lacking her wares; she decked the village hall
for whist drives, and the set bouquet supplied,
with fern bewhiskered, and with ribbon tied,

for Lady Lee who opened the bazaar.
The doctor, semi-centaur of a car
weather- and way-worn, subtle and obdurate
as he, was never known to pass her gate
without the purchase of a buttonhole.
She filled the chimney vase, the silver bowl
whose bright undinted cheek looked back the rife
wrinkles of Fanny Grove, a virtuous wife
for five and twenty years, and polishing still,
and the cracked teapot on the window sill
of sluttish, sickly, smiling Jenny Prince,
of all save love of flowers deflowered long since.
Gentle and simple, shamed and proud, she served:
to her the wantwit's cumbered footsteps swerved,
and Mrs. Hawley of The Bungalow—
who worshipped flowers, but couldn't make them grow—
bought week by week wellnigh a bottle's-worth.
Summering visitors, who found that earth
untutored but such simple toys purveyed
as died on being plucked, increased her trade
and spread her fame so far from coast to coast
that she was asked to send off flowers by post.

Her blossoms capped like foam the making tides
that heaved the graveyard mould, and went with
    brides
to church; pulpit and lectern, font and pew,
they trimmed for feasts, and the long weekdays
    through,
on the unvisited close air their breaths
exhaling, kept Christ company with their deaths.
    All this for gin. Yes, as you say, all this
for ransom, ease, illusion, the sole kiss
lorn age can trust to, the last kindness done
bewintered flesh that has outgrown the sun.
O faithful bottle!—whose dispassionate lip
pours to the solitary fellowship,
whose borrowed blood abhors not nor disdains
to live awhile along the dullard's veins,
whose weaving peace into the harassed mind
mounts a sweet trickster, skilful to unbind
the galling knots and cords of here and now—
thou art no niggard, and no chooser, thou!
At the first wooing yielding all thy fire
thee not the longest love can wholly tire.

None too uncomely are, nor commonplace,
for thee to greet; thou wrappest up disgrace
in the same mantle of oblivion
that feasted honour puts so warmly on.
Good fortune's fellow, by old ties invoked,
adversity beholds thee unreproached.
Mistrust salutes in thee the only fair
that will not play him false, nor is despair
quite without hope, commending himself to thee.
O courteous bottle, humbled to a fee!
and wearing amongst humankind such crass
constraints as those they bid thee awhile unloose.
    So, drinking flowers, Rebecca drank content.
But now no longer to the inn she went,
where all she saw, the ceiling smoked with soot,
the tramped-out oilcloth roses underfoot,
the beer-ringed table and the almanack
telling what moons lit nineteen-twelve, brought back
too shrewdly memories of former drought;
of evenings when the rain splashed down without,
and all, even the earth, might drink but she;
who creditless sat among the company,

and dully fawned, and heard the pendulum,
sneering and calm, go adding up the sum
of time twitched from her hope that one of these,
if not from kindness, from contempt, might please
to lean from Abraham's bosom to her lip.
Those who can buy whole bottles soon outstrip
the common tavern cheer of such as wrench
their ease from sitting crowded on a bench,
while draughts incessant round their ankles chide,
and a coarse closing time waits just outside.
Closing time, pooh! What was it now to her?—
a sweet alarum and remembrancer
to fill again, a vagrant nightly story
that passed, and left her midway in her glory.

    "There sits Rebecca, grown too proud to souse
but with her cat," said they. A new carouse
pride taught her, who from lonely drinking drew
deeper delighting, and a mystic grew.
Order, solemnity, and ritual
beseemed her drinking, and at each nightfall
she like a priestess trod the kitchen floor.
The blind must be drawn down, and locked the door,

the lamp well-trimmed set on its crochet mat,
plumped up the cushion, and shut out the cat,
and sometimes she'd wash hands, and comb her hair.
Meanwhile the bottle, so she was aware,
watched from the keyhole of its cupboard shrine.
While yet in darkness it began to shine
self-lit, and tingled with awakening fire,
and bulged its conscious flank to her desire.
And fetched, and poured, with its own ardour tame,
into the glass the meek and mastering flame
lapsed with what suppleness, with what silken pace
cringed up the bowl, and to itself a grace
before drinking murmured, until being come
to the brim it lay for very rapture dumb.
Harmless as any bride it lay, and wooed
her down with stillness; lip would be too rude
to crash against such crystal, sense too meagre
such an awaiting promise to beleaguer—
it should be possible not to drink but drown!
Slow the invincible circle wooed her down,
until the smell encountered, living and rank,
struck like a wave, and drowned her, and she drank.

So meek untasted, what a termagant
thrust its wellmet against her tongue, with rant
and dance and riot through her veins deployed!
Oh, this was youth, and youth must be enjoyed
roughly, for youth is short! How shall the rose
have joy of its brief petals if there blows
no wind to scatter them? Ravish the glass!
For youth is short, and shorter yet, alas!
this revenant wildfire conjured from the ash,
this pixie-light dancing on rotting flesh.
Make haste, make haste! Not even liquor may
burn long thus bright in the candlestick of clay,
nor pipe old mutton back again to lamb,
nor cheat your wise threescore. And though you swam
in drinks tonight, and sweet, you would not taste
another glass like this. Make haste, make haste!
  Fill up once more, Rebecca. Though the first
glass will not come again you have your thirst
still with you, and the night before you spread
deep and obsequious as a feather bed.
How well the steadfast lamplight fills the room!
How all the sights of everyday assume

44

what shapes of quaint reality! How wise
a countenance the clock's, how point-device
the row of cups along the dresser hung,
which seem to hang in air! And though the young
may think they own content, they only glance
at it, who round their painted maypole prance.
What pleasure theirs, on whom pleasures are dealt
violent as an August thunder-pelt,
that smites upon the field, but leaves it dry,
and presently is in a mist gone by?
How shall their liquor scrambled-down be matched
with the embalming fervour you have hatched
from your advised and contemplative booze?
Savour it well, sip cunningly, nor lose
one feather's weight of the enormous joy,
fixed on whose mounting tide you bob and buoy;
while round you chairs and pots and pans, entrapped
into such looks of stillness as the rapt
landscape of heaven wears, corroborate
by their continuance your blest estate.

    Youth you have pledged; that's gone; along your veins
nuzzles the toast to age; a third remains—

a deeper glass. How deep the night has grown!
At such an hour to such as drink alone
a guest arrives, with pomp and mystic riot
travelling from India. Out of the quiet
he mounts, he looms, he marches, and the blood,
in the ears' watchtower, with its rub-a-dub
drums his approach, and at his menie's shout
air whets its shrillest silence all about.
Fill to this guest, Rebecca, drink once more!
How soft his leopards pad your kitchen floor!—
and with their thick tails buffet you, and thresh
sharp waves of joy along your drowsy flesh.
Lovely they are, and affable, and tame,
and fawn and sidle round you, as the flame
fondles the log, owning you one on whom
their lord looks kindly. In your shabby room
how vast and calm a shade his ivy throws!—
dusky as wine out-poured, and to repose
weighing the thoughts of them who sit secure
in its inviolable clear-obscure.
Steeped in that shadow, sit, Rebecca, long!
Lost to the world, to you all worlds belong;

your bartered being, for the glowing ghost
that in this hour apparels you, well-lost,
and by this hour, that in an hour must hence,
even for its very fleeting recompensed.
Sit long, and deepen to the triumphing tide
that surged about an island and a bride;
drink onward, in this visiting glory arrayed
by him to whom your darkened vows were paid.
Drink the bright leopards, and the sacred shade!

  As moorland farmers drive their wedge of tilth
into the waste, outwitting with stern stealth
the casual might around their sally laid,
Rebecca set her husbandry to invade
the waste of winter. On till the first frost
the field was hers, but in a night was lost.
Against this iron, what could her annuals do—
her summer soldiers, who had wantoned through
an easy warfare since the first of May?
Mauled and dispersed the sixpenny squadrons lay,
their vigour bruised, their flaunt wilted and burned,
their fatness to a dismal jelly turned,

47

until the traitor sun, who was their friend,
smote with his midday scorn, and made an end.
Sad as a broken bottle was the sight;
and she through many a chilled and sober night
sat studying for a scheme to countervail.
Next year she planted honesty, whose frail
undaunted bucklers silver at the blows
of frost but yet hold out, and monthly rose,
whose scarlet not the longest night benumbs,
and tinfoil asters, and chrysanthemums.

   These last-fruits proved the best of all her gear
for autumn is a dying time of year,
and those who mourn, and feel the world's eye fixed
on their lament, don't hesitate betwixt
this penny and that, but spend as lavishly
as though each week would bring a legacy.
Even the dying, from whose hearts had died
all other passions, felt a stir of pride
forecasting all the braveries whose date
hung upon theirs; as in the old estate
of kings, entombed with such a retinue
of tributary deaths, it seemed they drew

toward no victor's but an equal's court.

Love Green knew this. And so when the report
that Mrs. Merley and old Isaac Hay
were both near death enriched a winter's day,
the common voice enquired, "What will they do?
Rebecca won't have flowers enough for two."
Long was the contest, for, intensely prayed,
death like a simpering girl his choice delayed.
The rival houses with defiance met,
stoutly dissembling an unfeigned regret
to hear new tidings of less hope; all ranged
to sides, and bets and bulletins exchanged,
while in this losing game for vantage lost
fretting, the sufferers, in their balance tossed,
envied each hearsay pang the other bore.
Only Rebecca, numbering her store
of present blooms and bottles yet to come,
preserved a courteous equilibrium.

What though the patriarch was stale in vice,
renowned for ancient rape and present lice,
and Bet had held her head up with the best
until her seventh bit her in the breast

49

and graffed a cancer there?—to neither cause
she leaned, death's partisan, not his or hers.
Why should she draggle to the strife impure?—
her gin was sure as death, and death was sure.
One should be taken—so the Holy Writ
avouched, and her impartial fancy knit
the wreaths, and to a grave in blank dispatched.
Meanwhile some wayside profit might be snatched.
Of either faction the ambassadors
she welcomed, and conducted them indoors,
parried the devious hint, and took the bribe
before the indifferent witness of her tribe
of housed chrysanthemums, englobed and bland
as fireside cats musing on creamjugs, and,
while they yet gloated, whisked them from the view
with a deft, "Well, I'm sure I feel for you.
But the poor soul—who knows?—may yet be spared."
A poor soul was. For while his backers declared
that Isaac would not see the morrow's sun,
Bet Merley, bandaged in oblivion
of morphia, moaned and vomited and died;
nor knew in her departure the wished pride

of dying first, but into Sheol passed
defrauded. "He laughs loudest who laughs last,"
her rival said, hearing the death-bell send
the news, and from that hour began to mend,
and called for meat, but called in vain, for all
his house were gone to see the burial.

DARK was the day, and vexed with coming storm.
The mourners shrugged and shuffled to keep warm,
and gathered their cheap sables closer round.
A southwest wind strewed dusk upon the ground,
and delved the shadow of the open grave.
Borne on its wings the tramp of the sea wave
tolled through the sentences, and in the gale
the vicar's surplice rattled like a sail.
Leaf on last leaf whirled through the creaking air,
the cypress writhed its summit like despair.
Pale and aghast the headstones gathered near;
pale and aghast, as though a mortal fear
had quenched their living white, bedaubed with clay,
tumbled on the cold ground, the garlands lay,
and heard the doom of man as though their own

51

pronounced: *He cometh up, and is cut down
like*—and the wind went by and snatched the word
and scattered it upon the air unheard.

Was this the end indeed?—would not death's clutch
spare even these fine flowers that cost so much?
So thought the widower: though he'd buried Bet
the wreaths might keep a little longer yet,
and do him honour, were they but housed fast
out of the weather till the storm were past.
At graveside lingering till all were gone
save Dennie Foot the sexton shovelling on,
he nudged his arm, and spoke, but nothing loud,
and pointed to the wreaths, and to the cloud,
and to the porch; and Dennie slapped his pocket
and cried, "Don't fear. I shall be sure to lock it."

The grave was filled, the sods rammed down awry—
so soon the impatient darkness took the sky,
knocking day on the head as though day were
a crack-legged rabbit squirming in a snare.
People withindoors, by the fireside brave,
were glad they were not lying in a grave
on such a night; even Rebecca, not

much given to fancy, thought how poor a lot
was hers who in this nightfall must be gone
to a new house, and settle in alone.
—A moping thought. . . . It would not let her be;
it watered down her gin as weak as tea,
and dimmed the flaring lamp, and hollowly spoke
within the chimney-breast, and puffed with smoke
into the room, and stared from the bereft
green indoor bower that had no blossoms left.
Let them be gone! She had their price instead!
She poured it in her lap, and dull as lead
it sank on her, and wearily as clay.
What ailed the gin tonight?—as well drink whey!
It had no power, no fire. Let the wind roar,
come such a storm as never came before,
she'd to the *Hand and Roses*, and buy more.

STRANGE was the night, and strange the road well-
    known;
everything strange, as though the wind had blown
thin the substantial world; and still it blew.
In the close tap she saw the things she knew,

heard casual greetings, and her own reply,
as though she were some traveller standing by,
whose glance, exact and unconcerned, sees plain
the seen-by-chance and never seen again.
　　When she set out for home the moon was up.
It shone in heaven like a brimming cup;
unspilled in all the turmoil of the storm
smoothly it hastened through the jostling swarm
of clouds that snatched at it. With a pale fire
it brimmed before her, stinging her desire,
so that she laughed aloud, and hugged the freight
of her four bottles, where inviolate
under the dark slumbered a fire that soon
would brim her full and merry as the moon.
Now by the church she passed, and a whim took
her mind to visit the new grave, and look
once more upon her flowers. Aye, and she'd show
the bottles forth to them, that they might know
they were not plucked, and thrown to earth, and taught
the lesson of a winter night for naught.
　　The gate clanged to behind her, and she stepped
into a dream. The blanched earth was so swept

with a black lightning where the elm trees tossed
their shadows that the look of graves was lost.
Scythed by that dark they crumbled and reshaped,
were, and were not, hollowed themselves and gaped
before her feet, and in an instant reared
back to reality. Onward she peered,
and as she went, grave after grave was twitched
out of her sight as though she were bewitched.
It must lie hereabouts. Not this. The next.
The next, then. 'Twas the shadows that perplexed
her pathway, and the frantic moonlight poured
in the brief interval the clouds restored
that blotted out with its extremity
of light the whiteness where her wreaths must lie.
Not this; the next. Not this; not this . . . she found
her footsteps stumbling at the new-made mound
that covered Bet. Raw it heaved up, as mean,
lank, and undecked as she in life had been.
Gone! Not a petal left. The flowers were gone!

Still mocked the moon, and still the wind raved on.
Deep within her dumbfounderment there stirred
The echo of a prophecy, a word

of flowers, that with double meaning would menace
man too: *The wind goeth over, and the place*
thereof knows it no more. Down fell the dark.
The moon was gone, blown out, a dwindled spark
receding through interminable cloud.
She clenched her limbs to shriek her loss aloud,
but in the gale's dominion words came not.
And wherefore shriek, and shriek to whom? And what
loss should she howl for, and what thief accuse?
And what this loss that was so deadly to lose?
Cry for a mess of flowers, and blame the wind?
No, it was more, was more!—and her robbed mind
knew itself sickening over an abyss
where all must to unreason sink if this
moment of loss were not revoked. She knelt,
and pawed and searched the grave, but only felt
heaped earth, and sticky clods, and shrivelling grass.
Robbed and betrayed! Down there the felon was,
who with her dead hand could reach forth to blight
flowers out of being. Always one for spite
was Bet, and even a corpse she'd have her will.
Ah, cunning one, couched there so snug and still,

where are those wreaths that you have filched away?
Answer me, or I'll rout you from your clay,
unkennel you, while I have nails to scratch
and breath to cry Halloo; I'll be your match,
for all your death, and all your powers of death!
Close to the grave she spoke; and from beneath
travelling through the·ground, answered a sigh.
  Waveringly it breathed, yet the outcry
of tempest could not tread it underfoot;
failing, it left a silence absolute
as though the last wave trembling to the shore
of time had come, and lapsed for evermore.
What, must it cower away with nothing told?—
a listless mockery beneath the mould?
Was there no engine to compel the dead?
Suddenly, all the churchyard was bespread
with moonlight, and the net of shadow blithe
as ever capered under boughs a-writhe.
Noosed in that net a glittering something grinned,
and beckoned her; unparcelled by the wind
the bottles lay, and to their mistress blinked.
On her illumined mind they shone distinct—

the sought-for engine, the awakening trump
that should uprouse the sleeper from her dump
and warm her lips to speech. Let her but taste,
and she'd tell all. On a tombstone in haste
she cracked a bottle neck, and pledged, and poured.
Over the sod with trickling pace explored
the gin, and sank, mouthed by the greedy clay.
But mute and glum the mannerless drinker lay;
and the first bottle, drinking turn about,
was drained, and cast, a dead-man, down, to flout
death's other wastage, and a second broached,
and well-nigh quaffed, before a sigh reproached
the air, as dragged out of a heart constrained,
and loath and wearily a voice complained.

"What is this talk of flowers? No flowers are here."
"Yet sorrowing neighbours laid them on your bier."
"Neighbours I have who nothing feel for me."
"In course of time they'll grow more neighbourly."
"Time may the living ease; us it helps not."
"You should lie easy now, your cares forgot."
"My cares were me. While I endure, so they."
"Aye, you'd a mort of troubles in your day."

"And seven my womb drove out, like days to know."
"The seventh was avenged on you, if so."
"Life grinds the axe, however we may end."
"Are all the dead doleful as you, my friend?"
"How are the living? Look in your own heart.
Farewell."
              The voice was gone. But like a dart
it stuck fast in her mind, and would not out.
The wind's incessant clamour could not rout
it from her hearing, nor the inward thud
of her alarumed and embattled blood
tread out its permanence. Cowed as a slave
who hears the whip she sat upon the grave,
but knew not where she sat, nor why she clutched
a bottle; blind, she saw the moonlight smutched
with vapour, and the trees, that groaned for pain,
toss back to grapple with the wind again;
and uncomplying, felt herself alive.
Why must she live, and why must all things strive
counter to endless onslaught, and the stress
of the long gravitational weariness
that bids all to the ground? Better at once—

since soon we must—lie down, and the strife renounce.
Yet did we so, little were mended by it.
Bet's seven would rage on, though Bet lay quiet;
nor could she, mated to the earth, keep long
her long virginity, for worms would throng
the city of her corpse, and whatso their
capacity, its fill of living bear,
and the weak grass thrust from her mound to quail
before the anger of another gale.
What sucked this life forth? What insatiate drouth
held evermore creation to its mouth,
and drank the human hurt like a sharp wine?
And that full moon, which she beheld so shine
and brim unspilled through cloud—what hand unseen
toward what terrible thirst bore its serene
renewing draught? Drunk as a lord must be
the Lord of heaven and earth! He, it was he,
who in his bottomless mixed cup pell-mell
poured all things visible and invisible;
who feasting drank the wind, and to the worm
stooped down his lip; whose revel had no term,
whose thirst unquenched begot its own allay

unstemmed, who was inebriate with clay,
with flowers, with fire, with the slow diamond squeezed
from time, with tigers, and the never-eased
genital pain, and the fixed Indian snows;
into whose cup the stars like bubbles rose
and broke; who in immortal fury trod,
alone, the winepress, and drank on, a God.
    Drank! She could drink too, in her little time
be drunk as he, unquestioned and sublime,
aye, and surpass him. Fuddle as he might,
he could not drain his cellar in one night,
nor, bound in husbandry of omnipotence,
be drunk beyond his means and damn the expense.
She, in this winter midnight, in this place
of death, fit tavern for one of mortal race,
with her two bottles left her, and the drear
unblossomed months of soberness drawn near—
patient as wolves, and grim, and sure—their threat
confronting and transcending to a whet,
would teach this God a lesson how to drink.
Let him look down, and envy her, and slink
crest-fallen back to his eternity!

And in this exploit of mortality
she, with her mite, to be magnanimous
as he with all his might, befitted. Thus,
as from his cup driblets of glory run
through man, to that slighted and sorry one
who lay beneath a wassail should abound:
had she more gin, she would stand drinks all round.
So would she revel out her night; so pull
down to her lips the brimming, bountiful,
gin-coloured moon. Already it stooped low,
swam, swooned towards her, warmed her with its
    glow
even in this night of chill. Nearer it swooned—
Now it was two! Two bottles, and two moons!
Quick, glass on stone! The dead in their neglect
would stir for doom, so shrill the bottle cracked. . . .

THE coroner summed up as you'd expect:
Drink is a failing which the state deplores.
If drink you must, then please to drink indoors.
    Such was his gist. He then grew fatherly,
opined the jury would be glad of tea,

and with the air of one who's cleared a botch
went with the doctor for a double Scotch.
The empty bottles brought as evidence
to show the cause of death were carried hence
by Mr. Merley as a perquisite.
Comfort he needed in his widowed plight;
comfort they gave; for added to the tale
of those his wife had emptied in this vale
of tears they brought the total to the exact
sum of his years and hers—a striking fact,
and manifesting clearly to his mind
cosmic arithmetic at work behind.

    Diversely scheme we the creative plan.
Olivia Drumble, who was anglican,
perplexed her spouse with talk of sacrilege,
God's acre, and what not. Meanwhile God's hedge
suffered a serious breach, where cognoscenti,
thinking it best to make a private entry,
crawled in to snuff about Bet's grave, and snare
the rich embalming odour lingering there.
For a full week the sods breathed out a smell
unmatched—mortality had spiced it well—

but with time's handling lost the lovely wraith,
and yielded, even to the nose of faith,
a smell like any other grave; like hers,
whose frolic death bequeathed the villagers
a tale that flashed awhile, and presently
waned, and was laid aside, extinct as she.
None broke a twig to view that resting-place.
Her legatees shrugged off the brief disgrace,
and with a briefer hope the name of Christ
bought on a label reasonably priced.
A larger label, saying: "To be Sold
this Eligible Property Freehold,"
bleached for a twelvemonth over the green neglect
that had been flowers, till fate chanced to direct
a couple by. "This is the place," said they.
"It's picturesque, and stands on the highway.
That green stuff cleared, gravel put down, some quaint
checked curtains, and a lick of orange paint,
and within-doors some mugs and warming-pans—
this is the very cottage of our plans."

 I passed the cottage some few weeks ago.
Where once the flowers had been there was a row

of tottering iron tables where no one sat.
Couched in the hedge I saw Rebecca's cat.
Out of the lifeless house there brayed a hoarse
aerial voice announcing cricket scores,
and a lean lady watched me loiter by
with a discouraged but attentive eye.
Beside the threshold where no traveller calls
a painted board said: "Teas and Minerals";
and at the inn I heard it told that these
newcomers did so poorly with their teas
that they had set out cots, one in the pantry,
to house the well-dowered by-blows of the gentry.
   I wish I had not gone that way, to smear
with aspect of the present the once clear
image of other summer when I first
saw the brave garden, and was told how thirst
had planted it. Then on Love Green I looked
as children on an open story-book,
and the best-painted picture it could show
was still Rebecca's stratagem a-blow.
Now from the page the picture blurs and dims,
wavers, discolours, perjures itself, dislimns.

The flowers are withered, even from my mind,
their petals loosed, their scent gone down the wind;
and she, to whom they such allegiance bore—
I knew her once, and know her now no more.